chicago bulls

portrait of an era

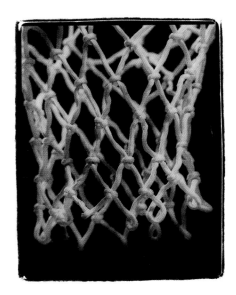

photographs by Barry Elz

text by Mark Vancil

photography and picture editor

Barry Elz

executive producer

V. Carlos Rojas Cardona

published by

Tango Publishing International Inc.

312 North May Street, Suite 5E, Chicago, IL 60607

writer, editor and project coordinator

Mark Vancil

designer

Georgia Bockos

designed and produced by

Rare Air, Ltd.

1711 North Paulina Street, Suite 311, Chicago, IL 60622

distributed by

Benchmark Press

A division of Triumph Books

601 South LaSalle Street, Chicago, IL 60605

special thanks to

my friends and co-creators of this book; V. Carlos Rojas Cardona,

Alberto Rojas Cardona, Mark Lind, Bob Wolgemuth, Chip Williams and Bill Babich at Tango Publishing.

Mark Vancil, Jim Forni, John Vieceli and everyone at Rare Air.

Tom Smithburg, for his tireless efforts, and Steve Schanwald at the Chicago Bulls.

and most importantly to the unparalleled Chicago Bulls athletes whose indomitable spirit on the court

has given us all so many unforgettable memories.

thanks to my family for their faith and support in all of my endeavors:

my parents, Javier and Areli, my brothers and sisters, Rocio, Javier, Gabriel, Arturo, Leticia, Sandra, Juan Jose, Alberto and Elisa.

carlos

chicago bulls portrait of an era

© 1998 Tango Publishing International Inc.

ISBN 09663572-0-5

◉

for my family
whose faith allowed this journey;
my wife, Carolyn and our kids,
Derek, Zach, Max, Noah,
Josh and Mavis

◉

BME

barry elz

Never have more words been used in more combinations to capture the brilliance of so many. Though their personas were established on basketball courts, the Chicago Bulls long ago transcended the game they play. Their individual schedules are packed tight with practice, appearances, commercial shoots, private excursions, doctors, therapists, games, planes and a measure of rest. They are rock stars with no backstage. ● Shooting intimate portraits of perhaps the century's most public sports personalities was not unlike jumping on and off a speeding train. The shoots were set up at the team's practice facility, the Berto Center. Our crew of five manipulated equipment, set materials hours on end, often without any knowledge of whether a scheduled appointment would be kept. ● We used Hasseleblad cameras with Speedo lighting gear. We hung steel panels dislodged from a scrap metal yard. We created an alternate set in the corner of a room using rough plaster walls and an old window from an architectural artifacts shop. We created a private studio complete with its own ceiling on site with 12-foot black curtains and mountain stands. ● The process started as much as four hours before a player, often sweat-soaked from practice, ambled into our area. Shoots lasted as little as five (Scottie Pippen) and as long as 45 minutes (Luc Longley). ● The challenge, spiked by the swirl of so many lives, was to capture these very public men in a collection of carefully crafted private portraits in a time frame condensed by fame. In the end, what they gave to me was not unlike what they give to thousands every night. But I got them when nobody else was looking. In those rare moments, when the train actually seemed to slow, they allowed me to capture a moment that otherwise might have blown by without notice.

 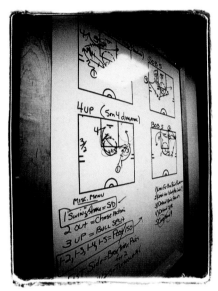

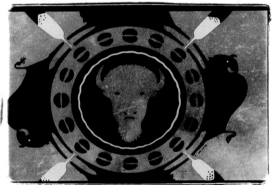

The moment violated base tenets of
the religious and spiritual teachings Phil Jackson
had encountered throughout his life.
And yet the man who later would ply his knowledge
of Zen Buddhism and American Indian spirit
to a brilliant conclusion on a group of unsuspecting
professional athletes was elsewhere. In the spring of 1978,
with his New York Knicks a game away from being swept
out of the playoffs by Philadelphia, Jackson coldly dismissed
the extended right hand of an opponent.
The Buddha within Phil Jackson had been buried by a form of
social engineering specific to sports where victory
defined success and losing defined all else.
But that brief encounter also came to define
the Phil Jackson who arrived in Chicago nine years later.
Jackson's awareness, the middle road calm fundamental to Zen,
and his acceptance of impermanence,
another building block of Buddhism, had become blocks of
his own foundation. That he called his opportunity
to coach the Bulls "a miracle for me, personally,"
seems eerily consistent with his philosophical revelation in 1978.
The opponent then had become the benefactor now.
Doug Collins, the 76ers guard whom Jackson had snubbed
in the heat of a basketball moment,
was the head coach Jackson replaced in the cold blow
of a business decision.

phil jackson

bill cartwright

Rivalry always has been a gentle way of explaining the obsession Patrick Ewing and the New York Knicks have with the Bulls.

On some level the fixation no doubt intensified with each championship ring Bill Cartwright acquired.

In the mid-1980s Cartwright had become a non-moving target for the New York media. A broken foot caused him to miss 162 of 164 regular-season games from 1984 to 1986 and earned him a variety of nicknames including Medical Bill. When Ewing was anointed the franchise savior in 1985, Cartwright slid even further out of favor. He had become a 20-minute a night back-up to Ewing when the Bulls decided they needed Cartwright more than they needed Charles Oakley. With Ewing in the middle and the relentless Oakley at power forward, the Knicks were elated.

Over the next five seasons, however, Cartwright became essential to the Bulls dominance, over New York in particular and the rest of the NBA in general. The Bulls won three championships.

The Knicks reached the Eastern Conference Finals once.

j i m m y
rodgers

The last time Jimmy Rodgers sat on a bench alongside Phil Jackson, it was Jackson taking the orders.

If what goes around comes around, something Jackson would call Karma, then it's only appropriate the teacher has become the pupil.

Rodgers was an assistant to Bill Fitch at the University of North Dakota where a long-armed center

named Phil Jackson was the team's star.

The smooth skin and sparkling eyes

could be those of a man 25 years younger.

And why not? For the last 51 years Tex Winter

has been a basketball coach at the Division I or professional level.

Not many damaging ultraviolet rays make it into gymnasiums.

Winter was 65 when he joined the Bulls

and installed his famed Triangle offense.

Now 76, Winter's personal history is as unique as it is long.

He played junior college baseball against Jackie Robinson,

recruited North Carolina legend Dean Smith, who retired from coaching

in 1997, and was one of the top three American pole vaulters in 1947.

Save for a stomach injury, Winter probably

would have been on the 1948 U.S. Olympic team.

A tremendous all-around athlete, Winter played on

the USC basketball team with future NBA Hall of Famers

Alex Hannum and Bill Sharman. Unable to compete the pole vault,

where he had a personal best of 14-feet, 4-inches using a bamboo pole,

Winter became the first full-time assistant coach

at Kansas State University. Later, as Kansas State's head coach,

Winter lead the school to eight Big Eight championships

in 15 years, including a memorable victory

over rival Kansas and center Wilt Chamberlain

to win the 1958 title.

tex Winter

jim cleamons

Calm, courteous and positive, Jim Cleamons has had to call upon
all those attributes during a professional career that has bounced high and low.
He was a rookie on the Los Angeles Lakers team that won 69 regular-season games during the 1971-72 season and an NBA Championship.
A season later he was playing for a Cleveland team that lost 103 games in two years. More than twenty years after that,
Cleamons was one of Phil Jackson's key assistants when the Bulls erased the Lakers' mark by winning 72 games and a fourth NBA title.
In keeping with the rhythm of his career, Cleamons found himself in Dallas
a year later, coaching a Mavericks team
that lost 58 times.

john paxson

John Paxson signed a free agent offer sheet with the Chicago Bulls Oct. 29, 1985,

the same day Michael Jordan broke his foot in a game at Golden State. For most of the next three years, Jordan stood by Paxson

while a series of Bulls tried to shove him aside. Wes Matthews, Steve Colter, Sam Vincent, Michael Holton, Rory Sparrow and later B.J. Armstrong

were among those brought in to solidify the point at Paxson's expense. By the time the Bulls were ready to challenge

for a championship, however, Paxson's cold, competitive spirit had dominated all comers.

A string of crucial jumpers in Game 6 deflated the Los Angeles Lakers and cemented the Bulls first championship in 1991.

Two years later, Paxson's jumper with seconds to play in Game 6

at Phoenix clinched a third consecutive title.

CHICAGO BULLS

Media Access

6:00 - 6:45

NOTICE

CHICAGO
BULLS

CHICAGO
BULLS

**AUTHORIZED
PERSONNEL
ONLY**

steve **kerr**

25

scott **burrell**

Steve Kerr came into the world in the same place his father departed.

Born in Beirut, Lebanon, four months after fellow NBA player Rony Seikaly was born there,

Kerr was a college freshman when he lost his father to the violence of that ravaged land in 1984. But like John Paxson before him,

Kerr fought his own war to become a professional basketball player. Though Paxson never endured the kind of career-threatening injury

Kerr suffered during college, both players negated physical limitations by the imposition of passion and will.

Until he was injured midway through the 1997-98 season, Kerr had not missed an NBA game in more than four years.

According to his teammates, he also hadn't missed many interviews, which gave rise to

his nickname, "The Moth" for all the time spent around

the bright lights of television cameras.

Put Scott Burrell on an NBA court

and he blends in among the long arms and legs of his peers.

But imagine the 6-foot-7 Burrell standing atop a pitching mound just 60 feet, 6 inches from home plate.

That's exactly what the Seattle Mariners saw when they made Burrell a first-round pick in the 1989 amateur baseball draft.

Burrell decided to play basketball instead of climbing through baseball's back lots.

A year later, this time a fifth-round pick of the Toronto Blue Jays,

Burrell relented and pitched parts of three seasons in the team's farm system when he wasn't playing basketball

and attending school at the University of Connecticut. He remains the only athlete ever drafted

in the first round of two professional sports.

bill wennington
34

The Bulls have more than 21 feet of foreign talent —

Toni Kukoc and Luc Longley included — and Bill Wennington accounts for seven of them.

He also accounts for the vast majority of pranks played on his teammates. There are the usuals, late night knocks on the doors

of just about anyone unfortunate enough to have gone to sleep early and obnoxious voice mail messages.

Then there are the unusuals such as freezing a player's underwear.

Genuinely funny and always up for a laugh, particularly at the expense of someone who won't find the prank nearly as amusing,

Wennington is also accessible to everyone from fans to media. Indeed, Wennington has been known

to stay at team functions talking to people and signing autographs until after

the last catering employee leaves.

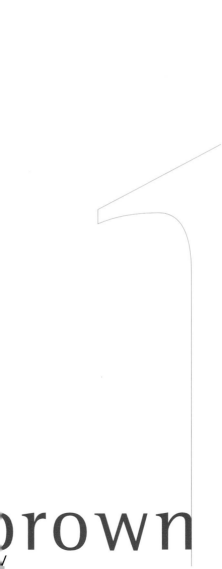

rown

Randy Brown wasn't born when his mother, Marie,

and father, Willie, moved north from Greenwood, MS, where Marie had been born on a cotton farm.

The fifth of six children, Randy grew up on Chicago's West Side.

Years later, as a 26-year-old point guard for the Sacramento Kings, Randy Brown made his move back to Chicago.

Intense and driven, Brown had worn down Kings starters and put himself in line for a starting job.

But Randy Brown wanted to come home. He traded regular minutes and a higher NBA profile for a seat near the long end of the Bulls bench.

For most, two championship rings might justify the move, playing time or not.

For Brown, being home always has been

the only justification necessary.

Before Brian Williams ran with the Chicago Bulls

he ran through the streets of Pamplona with real bulls. He has ridden a camel near Cairo.

He has read Kant and Kierkegaard. He plays the saxophone. He dabbles with the guitar. He is a licensed pilot and owns his own plane.

He helped the Bulls to an NBA championship after agreeing to play for the league's minimum salary.

He has played for five NBA teams in seven seasons.

He cried when he read Miles Davis' autobiography and realized his passion for basketball

didn't match the musician's passion for music.

His passion is elsewhere. Passion comes from the soul.

We all should be so fortunate.

◉

robert parish

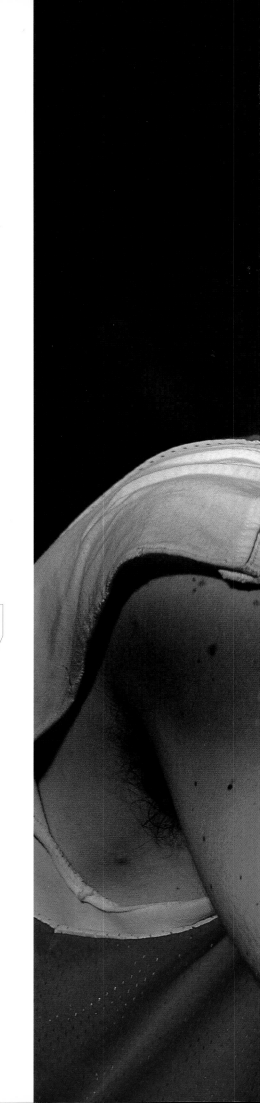

toni **kukoc**

7

If operations chief Jerry Krause had his way 22 years ago,

Robert Parish would have been a Bull for life and the Boston Celtics would have had to find another All-Star or two to surround Larry Bird.

Parish caught the eye of a number of NBA scouts during his career at Centenary College in Louisiana.

But Krause was one of the few who came to know Parish, later nicknamed "Chief" after the quiet Indian in "One Flew Over the Cuckoo's Nest,"

and understand the warrior inside the almost-stoic exterior.

As Bulls general manager for three months in the mid-1970s, Krause wanted Parish in the 1976 NBA Draft.

Ownership opted for Scott May. To some extent, that's why the Bulls were in the mess they were when Krause took over in 1985.

While the Bulls ran through centers such as Artis Gilmore, Dave Corzine, Jawann Oldam and Granville Waiters,

Parish became part of one of Red Auerbach's greatest trades — Parish and a first-round draft pick that turned out to be Kevin McHale

went to Boston in a deal with Golden State that translated into three NBA Championships in the six years.

Krause finally got Parish into a Bulls uniform in 1996 just in time

for another championship ring.

◉

Stories of his exploits crossed the ocean long before Toni Kukoc made the trip himself.

Years before Kukoc agreed to join the Bulls, Philadelphia 76ers coach Larry Brown told of a young, 6-foot-11 guard

splashing three-pointers on American collegians.

By 1993, Kukoc, then just 25, was considered the greatest player in the world outside the NBA.

But it was the lure of playing alongside Michael Jordan that convinced Kukoc to leave his beloved-but-war-ravaged Croatia

and pass up millions of dollars in Europe for the Bulls.

When Jordan announced his retirement just two days before training camp opened in 1993,

Kukoc, 5,000 miles away from home,

broke down and cried.

ron harper

9

Bags of ice melt slowly against the warm swell of Ron Harper's knees.

The routine, like the ache, was born of multiple surgeries seven years ago.

The operations, which reduced two seasons by half, might have reduced lesser people by at least that much.

But Harper long ago had dealt with a pain far more penetrating than anything an injury could inflict.

Once a high flying scorer and budding superstar, Harper accepted the new limits imposed by circumstance

and moved along just as he had done years before.

As a child, Harper had a severe stutter that belied

an unusually polished athletic talent. Despite a brilliant high school career on the court,

Harper's speech problems intimidated some college recruiters. When Miami of Ohio decided to take a chance,

Harper gathered himself and moved along. Four years later, his stutter largely conquered, Harper was an All-America forward

with a college resume that included work with the Special Olympics and local children's groups.

No longer able to attack the basket like he once did, Harper now defends the same.

Who knows whether it's the passion or the warm fluid

that floats around Harper's knees that turns

the ice into water?

No one has played more professional

basketball games in the 1990s than Scottie Pippen.

In addition to more than 650 regular season games,

Pippen has played in more than 115 playoff games and more than

25 games leading up to and including two Olympics.

He has earned two Gold Medals, played on five NBA Championship teams

and has been named an NBA All-Star eight times.

scottie **pippen**

Superman never had a partner

and neither did Michael Jordan until Scottie Pippen escaped the shadow of Jordan's cape.

Michael came first, his a shining example of excellence and integrity played out in a remarkable combination of consistency, courage and will.

Jordan once was cut from his high school basketball team,

Pippen's high school career led to a job as equipment manager at a small Arkansas college.

Jordan endured, Pippen grew.

Michael left the legend of Dean Smith and North Carolina for a gold medal

at the 1984 Olympics and then, the Chicago Bulls.

Pippen, deep in the shadows of his own existence

even as a college senior, came out of nowhere, almost literally, to be a top five pick in the 1987 NBA Draft.

Together, with five titles, four gold medals and 19 All-Star games between them,

they continue to play with the fearlessness that defines greatness.

They have become comfortable with the pain, the same pain that sidelines a multitude of their peers every season.

Look closely at their arms in midseason and the long, deep scratches mark the wars.

Their ankles swell, knees ache and tendons scream.

They arrived alone.

Together they advanced.

23

michael jordan

The show was built on fundamental athletic performance
and a piercing will. But not even the unique physical gifts
or the most-developed mental fortitude explain the consistent excellence
that has defined Michael Jordan on and off the court.
Indeed, no one in the history of sports and entertainment
ever has moved so smoothly and with such brilliance
between life and live performance.
He has written best-selling books, starred in a movie,
negotiated multi-million dollar deals with multi-billion dollar corporations,
juggled practice, interviews, commercial shoots and games
in the same day, moved the stock price of companies with whom
he does business, created a series of best-selling videos,
become a husband and three times a father and all along remained
among the most famous people in the world and the absolute
best ever at his profession. Ruth. Ali. The Beatles.
Were any of them ever as good as often
in as many facets of their lives?

9

d e n n i s
rodman

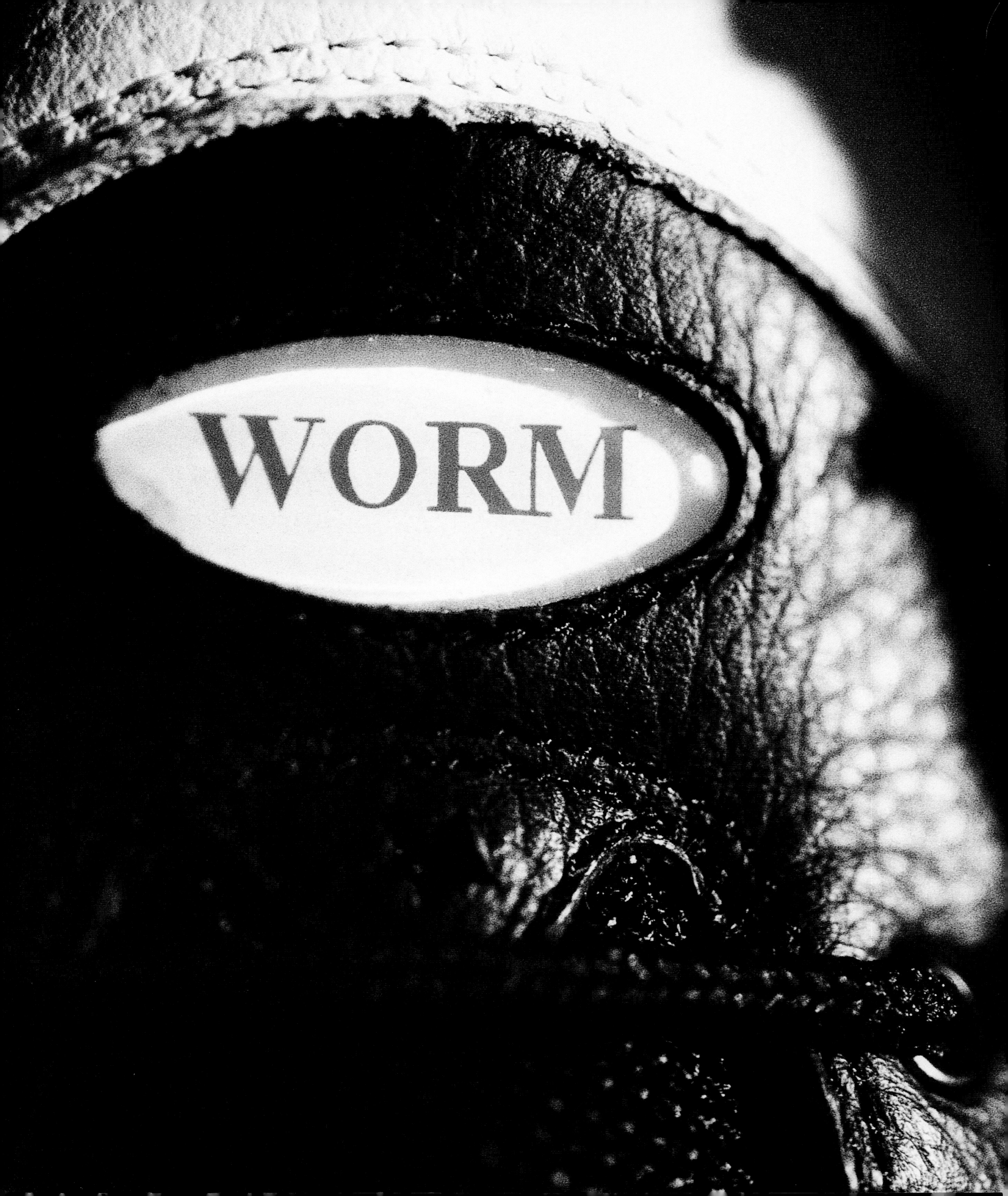
WORM

The swirls of color and dramatic lines
that form tattoos along Dennis Rodman's body
speak volumes for a man who often
has very little to say.
If the outside screams to be heard
amid the din of our cultural noise, the inside
often remains unto itself.
Within the contradiction is a rhythm that no doubt
always has been Rodman's alone. How else could a man
find peace amid a flurry of pointed elbows and deliberate shoves
by men often taller and heavier?
Does it surprise anyone that Rodman
always takes a shower before the game?
Or that he politely shook hands with the President
of the United States, disrobed and strode into the shower
as President Clinton addressed the rest of the team?
Or that Dennis often sits alone on the team plane
with a leather jacket pulled over his head as he sleeps?
What about the fact Rodman
sometimes lifts weights before a game,
during half-time and after games?
Others may pick up the beat,
but Rodman is the only one capable
of dancing to it.

luc
longley

13

Lucien James Longley sways

in the wind of criticism and praise without giving either much notice.

Though 7-foot-2, and nearly 300 pounds, Longley has an innate compassion.

Easy going and affable even to those he doesn't know,

Longley is as gentle as a giant can be in the NBA.

Ask him how he's doing and just about any time of the day

the Australian center responds with a smile,

"No worries, mate."

j u d **buechler**

dickey simpkins

8

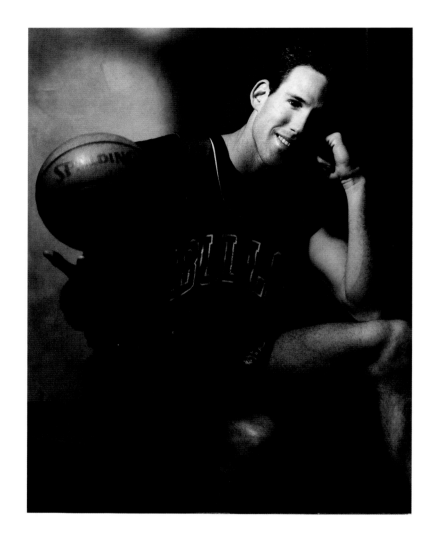

The knees have endured too many practices and too many NBA conflicts to go back now.

But Jud Buechler hasn't stopped wondering about what might have been.

He was 10 years old when his father, Don, a volleyball player and coach, introduced Jud to real competition on the Southern California sands.

An exceptional athlete at 6-foot-6, Buechler hasn't stopped returning to the beach game since.

He even played in a professional event in 1996 on Chicago's Oak Street Beach and remains

friends with the sport's top pros. For now, Buechler gets his surf and sand fix

from his favorite magazine, Longboard.

●

He might be the least-famous player on the most-famous team in the world,

a silent spot with an artist's bent in what is otherwise a rolling thunder review. Had he been louder, funnier, or simply better,

Dickey Simpkins might be associated more closely with the team that drafted him in 1994.

As it is, Simpkins, a quiet and decent man, is best known for being the 13th man on a 12-man team.

Left off three consecutive playoff rosters, Simpkins was dealt to Golden State before the 1997-1998 season and then, inexplicably,

returned to the Bulls for Jason Caffey, whose ability helped bury Simpkins in the first place.

Perhaps it's the artist in Simpkins that allows him to go so placidly

amid the storm of his own career.

35

jason caffey

joe kleine

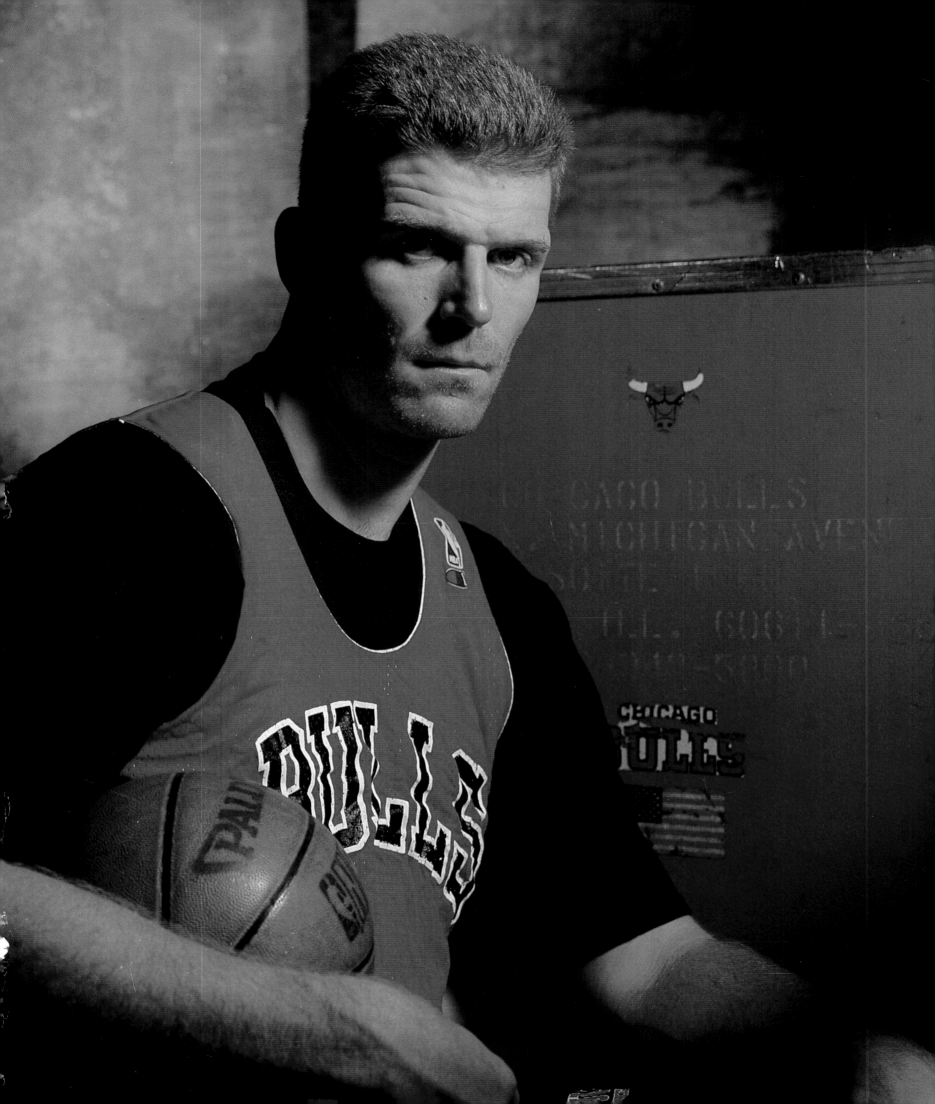

The University of Alabama is a football school and although
Jason Caffey went there to play basketball, former coach Gene Stallings, who had played for Bear Bryant, was looking for a tight end.
The same package that caught the eyes of the Chicago Bulls in the 1995 draft first made an impression on Stallings.
At 6-foot-8 and more than 250 pounds, Caffey has the kind of hands, quickness and speed
college football coaches spend years trying to locate.
Caffey avoided Stallings, blended into a front line that featured Antonio McDyess and still
is trying to become the kind of power forward NBA general managers
travel the globe trying to discover.

Joe Kleine walked into the Chicago Bulls offices for the first time in 1985.

By the time he left, the future of the franchise was in danger of being transformed.

A year earlier, Kleine had teamed with Michael Jordan on the 1984 U.S. Olympic Team. And now, with the 1985 NBA Draft just weeks away,
operations chief Jerry Krause wanted to confirm his infatuation. "A taller version of Jerry Sloan," is how Krause described the hard-working 7-foot Kleine.

Krause, however, could be forgiven for falling so hard. He had gone into the previous season with Dave Corzine, Jawann Oldman,
Steve Johnson and Caldwell Jones occupying the middle. But fate intervened early in the NBA draft when Sacramento selected Kleine with the sixth pick.

Krause maneuvered to land Charles Oakley instead. Three years later, with the Bulls still searching for a frontline center,
Krause shipped Oakley to New York for Bill Cartwright. By the time Joe Kleine made Chicago
his sixth NBA home, Cartwright had retired to the Bulls bench
with three championship rings.

◉

nba record

72

500

Reached 500 career victories in just 682 games,
faster than any coach in NBA history.

1

Ranks first in career scoring average,
more than a point ahead of Wilt Chamberlain.

6

Voted to the NBA All-Defensive First Team six consecutive seasons
entering 1997-98.

7

His NBA record seven consecutive rebounding titles,
including the 1997-98 season, are two more than any other player in history
and six more than any forward.

Jerry Reinsdorf is a CPA, lawyer, specialist in real estate securities, registered mortgage underwriter and certified review appraiser.
He never even had worked for a professional sports franchise when he became chairman of the Chicago White Sox in 1981. His qualification for that role,
other than a brilliant business sense, was the fact Reinsdorf loved baseball. Indeed, he was a fan.

But not even Reinsdorf has spent as much time at institutions of higher learning as Jerry Krause.
About the time Reinsdorf was finishing law school, Krause was traveling the country as a "scout" for the Baltimore Bullets in an era when NBA teams
rarely had assistant coaches, much less scouts. Krause's qualifications? He was a fan.

If they have anything else in common it's the general disregard for sentiment when it comes to making tough decisions.

Unlike legendary Red Auerbach, Krause has operated in a time of salary caps, free agency and the Players' Association.
But as Auerbach demonstrated once he left the Boston Celtics bench, in the NBA you only need to be right once or twice every few years to establish a legacy.
In Krause's case, four moves on the bench and four others in the locker room have defined his tenure and the championships that followed.

Krause hired Doug Collins, hired Phil Jackson, fired Doug Collins and then made Phil Jackson head coach.
On the court, Krause cleaned out a horrible roster in the early years, and built the foundation for titles to come in a single draft when he landed Scottie Pippen
and Horace Grant. Then he did the unthinkable when he traded Charles Oakley for Bill Cartwright. Getting anything for Stacey King,
much less a serviceable starting center in Luc Longley, is among a number of other relatively minor signings and maneuvers
that have kept the franchise moving forward.

But while the Bulls of Reinsdorf and Krause have won more championships
than every other professional franchise in Chicago added together, credit often has gone elsewhere.
The irony is that in a culture defined by mediocrity, Krause and Reinsdorf have been judged on style rather than substance.

The reality, however, is that in professional sports cold numbers and hard facts certify success and failure.
And in the case of the Chicago Bulls a once tired and struggling franchise has been transformed during the Reinsdorf-Krause era
with state-of-the-art facilities and five NBA Championships entering the 1997-98 season.